THE NIGHT WORKERS OF RAGNARÖK

THE
NIGHT WORKERS
OF
RAGNARÖK

KRISTJANA GUNNARS

Press Porcépic
Toronto/Victoria

This edition is published by Press Porcépic Ltd., 235-560 Johnson St.,
Victoria, B.C. v8w 3c6, with the assistance of the Canada Council.

Typeset by The Typeworks in Pilgrim 10/13
Printed in Canada.

Cover design by Seabrook and Bobolo Ltd.


**Canadian Cataloguing in Publication Data**

Gunnars, Kristjana, 1948-
    The night workers of Ragnarök

Poems.
ISBN 0-88878-240-3 (bound). — ISBN
    0-88878-239-X (pbk.)

I. Title.
PS8563.U56N5 1985    C811'.54    C85-091369-1
PR9199.3.G86N5 1985

*Acknowledgments*

The poems in this collection have appeared in the following journals:

"north country wake" and "bed of opium" in parts in *Contemporary Verse II*; *Poetry Canada Review*; and *NeWest Review*.
"wild waters" in *Prairie Fire*.
"milky way vegetation" in part in *Waves*.
"The Night Workers of Ragnarök" in part in *Northern Light*.
"stone bridge poems" in *Canadian Ethnic Studies*.
"milky way vegetation II" in part in *Women and Words: The Anthology*.

*for Gudrun, my sister*

# THE NIGHT WORKERS OF RAGNARÖK

# CONTENTS

# Introduction

The poems in this collection were written between 1981 and 1985. During this time I travelled between the old world and the new many times, and I had ample opportunity to speculate on homelessness, leave-takings and the loss of worlds. The series of poems included here were all prompted by different circumstances, and they are not connected. Yet, if there is anything that unites these poetic cycles, it must be what seems to have emerged as the "return of the native" syndrome. All but "wild waters" and "stone bridge poems" deal in some way with a return to the old country after acculturating in the new. The other two cycles concern themselves with the inverse situation of a return to the new country after readjusting to the old.

The "return of the native" theme is, however, only a jumping board for reflections of a wider sort. On looking back over these poems, I see they register a search for a kind of truth, and it is a truth imbedded in place. I cannot say for certain what I was looking for, but I know where I looked. Unfortunately, I am afraid this book of poems amounts to a record of what I did not find.

"Wild waters" was written after canoeing in Lake of the Woods, Ontario. If there is anything that epitomizes the nature of Canada, it is the act of silently gliding over such mirror-calm water and hearing the cry of a loon in the night. At such times, all human endeavors seem vain and insignificant, and I recall the feeling of relief in being free from the pressures to conform in European society. In what is perhaps the most ardent of truth-telling chronicles in the Western world, Jean-Jacques Rousseau says in his *Confessions* of 1770 that he "could no longer see any greatness or beauty except in being free...." That was how I felt returning to Canadian nature.

Rousseau also says that "in complete contrast to theologians, doctors and philosophers only admit to be true such things as they are able to explain." I had many doubts about the formal pursuit of learning, specifically, the doctorate of philosophy I undertook during these years. In an attempt to gain some distance from the university and to rethink my goals, I spent a summer in Iceland reading books and taking walks in the southern countryside. "Milky way vegetation" was written during those months, and there is much in the poems about the folly of ambition, although I do not say so directly. Even though I felt very much at home in the country of my origin, I was always aware that I had been educated out of that world, and there was nothing I could do about it in retrospect. In my academic attempt to become a "philosopher," I could not help feeling I had neglected the healthy regard for the unexplainable that characterizes Icelandic thought.

A year earlier, I made a kind of pilgrimage to Markerville, Alberta, where the Icelandic-Canadian poet Stephan G. Stephansson spent much of his life. It was in Stephansson's poetry that I found consolation for the feelings of absence I carried with me as an "immigrant." By "absence" I mean the sense that you are always *without* something essential; a fear that you have forgotten something important, or left a part of you behind. Stephansson answers this sense of loss with an urge for freedom, courage, and progress—the typical feelings that drove the western pioneers on into the unknown. But he voices these thoughts in a personal and biting way, never giving in to nostalgia or sentimentality. Markerville itself turned out to be one of the vanishing hamlets of the Prairies, and the only signs of life seemed to be a post office window, a blacksmith's shop, and a toymaker's garden. I wandered around the countryside looking at the fields and the foothills beyond, and realized, of course, that the pioneer history that shaped Stephansson's poetry was over. "Stone bridge poems" was written after this visit; I had in mind the reclining farm-buildings of the past, given over to wind and weather.

"Bed of opium" and "north country wake" were written during a winter of university studies, as I was trying to reassess the cruder aspects of my childhood culture. In that world of books and papers, there seemed to be an urge to recreate the memory of something more immediate, tactile, earthy and real. These two sequences of poems deal more than anything else with memory and loss. The world I lived in as a child is also history, for the old country has changed dramatically, and become modernized in the last twenty-five years. The question for me was, what does remain? Some of the pictures I word-painted must still exist, but, I feel most fundamentally, that it is the images of childhood that create the person you are, because you carry them with you for the rest of your life. I also wanted to focus on the pictorial in these poems, and somehow I kept recalling Vincent Van Gogh's "Dutch period," of heavy, dark, greenish-brown peasant paintings. I chose to picture that which was most ancient and remote.

In "the silent hand" I again returned to Iceland, and this sequence is specifically concerned with the whaling industry that has been carried on there over the centuries. I made an effort to reconcile my sympathies for the tradition of necessity, and what I had learned about conservation since I went abroad. I felt that in focusing on the whalers, I could more accurately depict the emotions with which I grew up. There was always a sense of bleakness, a fear of fate, and an overhanging premonition of death. What amazes me now is the readiness with which one was willing to accept death, for others as well as oneself. It seemed natural to die, and not at all bitter to die young. I felt that this unarticulated fatalism must have some cause, and I sought to discover the reason as I wrote the poems in this cycle. Death-stories abounded in the folklore we were fed as children, but mixed with the terror of mysterious events and dreams was a profound sense of comfort at the thought of going into that warm darkness. I think now that a people's emotional makeup is molded by necessity,

3

and the truth is that a fishing nation has to be prepared to accept a certain percentage of deaths on the fishing banks every season. It is a matter of chance who is chosen each time.

"The night workers of ragnarök" is the earliest of the series in this book. These poems were written during a year I spent in Iceland working as a journalist. I wrote much during that dark winter, feeling as though I had never left at all. I may have been influenced by Scandinavian poetry, which is dominated by a certain form of plain-speaking. The fascination with experiment in language and form that one often finds in modern Canadian poetry is not so evident there. What does amount to an obsession in Scandinavia, and which is woefully absent from Canadian letters, is a concern with global nuclear escalation. There has been talk of making the Nordic countries a nuclear-free zone, and discussion is constantly taking place on issues of world peace. I could not help noticing the insidiousness of the situation where a nation without armed forces, dedicated to peace, nonetheless cannot escape the effects of international nuclear escalation. In these poems I registered the daily life around me in Iceland as I saw it; people preparing their trawlers, hanging up stockfish, standing in the fish-plant processing the catch. Into this scene I inserted the early years of the atomic age. I wanted to tell the truth, not to force an issue. And it is Rousseau again who makes the distinction when he says, "my function is to tell the truth, not to make people believe it."

WILD
WATERS

**I**

so far the river
has shot by sharp
rocks, granite edges, this

has been pure white water
wilderness, always

roaring rapids a-
head, white spray on
the horizon, narrowing

drops in the rumbling
end:   then
the falls

so far the rock-solid river bottom has not cut me
off, but only so
far

**2**

i only wanted
the early dawn, land
of large, soft
water, to awaken before

morning, the violent
storm, the inclement time
of day, before the final

gem in a harrowing
dark sky
fades
i only wanted to lift the paddle

a moment upwards
rest it on the gunwhale in
the early hours

this is all

## 3

time now for wild waters
to still, life
becomes an old
friend, we take each other
for granted, learn
when a stream forks
to choose one

on shore, a pile-up
of broken ice, logs
branches, leaves, time
now for silence, to watch
the underwater weeds bend
waver by themselves, to be

alone

MILKY WAY
VEGETATION

**I**

i no longer love the grasses
and sedges at my feet
the common things
saxifrages, roses, daisies
on the ellidaá riverbank
below our city

the days have become a sky
where stars lie
a pocket watch of eternity
rough concentrations of gas and dust
imbedded in expectation

and i do not love the sky
dew at my feet
dim reflections of city lights
the river that meanders into nebulosity
i have lost them

**2**

we walked the gravel banks today
and found the river-bed dry

a broad-leaved willow stood
in the lowlands

and i thought of fate as a galactic belt
gliding distances from earth

the light-years between this moment
and the spectacular object of future

drifted between the loose stones
and wafting willow leaves

**3**

you stoop for the scented orchid
hold the lyngbye's sedge against your face

and i know the references charted now
will diffuse in portraits
dating the steps we took
and the wind blows

the smell of hay, orchid, sedge
lingers in the touch, your hand
pressed against my palm, the chart

they refer to as fate

**4**

i will leave you on the shore of a small lake
and as i vanish
i will see the land surrounding you
and you will stand alone
where blue felwort
flowers grow in the bog

absurdly i will plan for the skies
to live in ellipsoidal clouds
where every word is luminous
and poems are hot central stars
in cities of spherical gas

i plan to see the lake grow smaller
and smaller as i fly
and you will be the blue felwort
diminished by space

## 5

i have come to walk the coast with you
to restrict my life
within arctic soul

you discover for me parts of our country
alpine whitlow-grass
saxifrage and mountain heath

small disks resembling planets
exploding

we press these saxifrages with our boots
turn the little flowers
into debris of stars

i have not come to discover the midnight sun
but to destroy the flame
and explode summer

**6**

you temper my life
i notice the interesting species
exile no longer threatens to blind

the sword moss beyond the city
at kleifarvatn and krísuvík
where i pass year after year
in the curious geography of love

will be written in the annals
our worlds will be
alphabetical prefixes, little
more

the magnitude of this nebula
i see as suffering
will become a caption

the sword moss will be my companion
the future will give way
to curiosity

## 7

the lichens we recognize
in our common experience
the mountains of longing
the northern hemisphere we took to be our own

are not the friends i imagined

fate has become a milky way
of possibilities, spiralling
around this moment, mountains
of galaxies

pile up at my feet
lichens on the stones we lean against
provide a negative of space
distant, cold

**8**

the tenderness that grew over the winter
you planted here
between the coast and mountains of all i knew

and now the birch woods i look for
again are absent
you have cut them for fuel
you have brought sheep to graze

ours is a small scrubland

the similarities between us
the family resemblance
were planted distances away
measured in light-years

and there we speak of magnitude
and not of little feet in withering leaves
or axes among gnarled trunks

## 9

i will shelter this little wood
in the valley, vaglir and hallormsstadur
birches ten meters high

why should i not preserve
the rowans and tea-leaved willows
protect the dwarf shrubs
they are all we have left

i will hand-draw a map of this growth
check the positions of solitudes
as you identify constellations

observe the distances for fainter stars
try to see with the naked eye
vague hopes

sheltered among the grasses, find
perhaps a single herb
that went unscathed when we parted

MILKY WAY
VEGETATION II

**I**

you do not know if
i do not tell you, how
i see among the grasses

lady's bedstraw, wood
cranes' bills, water avens
and wild angelica

each one appears many times
a negative of constellations

how between the print and reality
i have placed you

standing in the hawkweeds
exposed under the sky

## 2

between dry stretches
covered with sedges
i have been through carpets of cotton-grass
in the central highlands

between tundra bogs
ridged with gravel and stone
i have been through grasslands
heaths scattered with plants

my journeys uncharted, undated
the boundaries unmarked
the hours broken
my uncoordinated life

## 3

a touch of the wild thyme
and moss campion of very old
mountain-drifted freedom
appears with you

who do not know
that with you the highlands occur
showing again the old sky
approximately as it would look

to the unwarned eye

**4**

even while the blue and red summer nights say yes
yes

the black sands follow me
the lowlands extend barren
newly-poured lava flows down the gullet of hope

and there is continuous no on the wings of the gulls

## 5

after this returning, i know

the beds of moss, dwarf
shrubs, birches
rained-on

ravines of ferns and herbs
luxuriant
brilliant red stars at my fingertips

life a glowing object

STONE
BRIDGE
POEMS

## summer awning

doors and windows stand exposed
to the glare of sun
in late summer

i am no longer at home
the summer awning on the old house
hangs in tatters

if i could live here
i would frame you
but here only the wild rye grows
with wide-open eyes to the sun
and white lines segregate my vision

you are too distant, but i would
introduce you to this
land eaten by cattle
if i could
and to my dreams eaten by late summer

i am here like the early autumn
unprotected against the merciless prairie
exposed
without the membrane of your pasture fields

your skin and claws
clasping the coarse winter
before it arrives

## cider vinegar

in the old days it was important
among the farm labourers
to keep a row of cider barrels
beside the beef and pork

they could dispense with nothing
and i have the nothing they left behind
a plain
narrow reed grass

smooth under the surface
all over in wet places

you do not know that old time
the truncate existence
simple and indistinct

but the past lives in you
because you barrelled the essence
like slaughtered blood
you showed me how to see the plain
and when i returned from you

i tore by the sheath
the round margins away
that should have shaped our lives

you showed me how to see the loss
marked in the long slender rhizomes
yellow and green in the dust

and where the cider of more careless days
spilled on the caked mud
i learned to know what withers

## Story

as the slender wood grass at my feet
i die
wide as the prairie
long, flat
as fine scabs of surface wounds
i am always absent
from your life and mine

but far in time i recall
the potato bread of childhood
woman boiling, mashing, sieving fruit of earth
warm overnight
childhood never reformed

brittle, i am
sifted in the memory
of woman's gestures
and then of your gestures

pour me with one hand
stir me forever—
i remember mothers of the past
sponges of the night
when i could feel

you would not take this cowboy story
of my life if i gave it
to love is costly
and here in the wood grass, gentle one
what do you know

## cuban watermelon

they say bugs eat the leaves and stalks
of watermelon, that the best
protection is a screen cover
of old newspapers
cut in pieces

when the watermelon grows the paper
rises and in the rain
it breaks open again

endless, the grower's pain
prostrate, the life
crowded conscience
rolled in the present over and over

that is the life of false buffalo grass
papery with hopelessness
prepared for no rains
and the memory is inflated with water

i am the cuban watermelon
broken again with memory
endlessly i leave what i have found
such as you

and in the newspapers you may read
your own story
in my obituary:
broken again
false to myself, rolled again

in the buffalo grass of the plains

## straw hive

honey boxes
with rain-shedding roofs, slanting
and clean straw packed in tight
bound with wire:

the bees were glad of the straw
cool in summer
warm in winter
they buzz under the house-apiary still
though the hive is gone

like winter
smoothed in the brome of time
the fields once kept bright red and blue
are dark green now
ribbed and veined with brome

the storm gathers dust
and i see you clearly in the brown distance
you too have been shed by time

but i was grateful for you then

the clean desire
to be bound in the wires of your arms
and the memory fades
the buzz of bees dies out

but i can watch them go forever

## smoky chimney

in the country house wing
when wind blew down the chimney
we saw smoke

how we devised against the sooty night
with caps of stone
bricks in the four corners
breaking the gust into a thousand eddies

the wind drove everywhere
up and down the flue
the house filled with smoke

now the june grass grows here
blue and green in the peace of morning
pale as the dawn haze lifts

see how the weeds crowd into the wing
where the country house half-
lies in its bones

how clear the chimney
dry with abandonment
a few roots, a few grass blades
straddle the dirt

how easy to forget as the wind blows
the black night
when we could hardly breathe
the world was too close for us

but you blow the pictures away somehow
your touch still drives the morning
and this will be another dream
to awake from

how easy to stand and walk
to breathe the warm comforting wind
after all

## stone bridge

the stone bridge stood fifty years
without repairs
here and there a stone displaced
flat stones engraved by weather

covered with a layer of earth
above the roadbed
large boulders stuck at the ends
and embankments that did not wash away

under ran the rapid stream
and beside the channel
early blue grass grew bristled

here is where orphaned infants sailed
through the narrow opening
under the bridge

you and i, like that
indistinct and white-veined
had this bridge to ourselves
in the midribs of the year

here lie the displaced stones
the weathered boulders
perched over a stream of running blood
that continues in my veins

unrepaired
our stone bridge has remained
unused for many dry days
and only the blue grass whispers any of this aloud

# dwarf pear

there were trees budded
kept small
short-lived:   unprofitable, they said
unworthy

they were garden dwarf trees
high-culture trees
made with hours of judicious pruning

i remember fathers gathering
the easy flourish of many years
loaded with fruit
a year from the bud

fathers who argued the incessant success

i lie in the manna grass again
remember those tall sayings
and how easily my thoughts rupture
how fast you flow out

the sloughs of loss:
was our culture then not coarse enough—
how miniature we kept our love
how we erased the wet meadows

and when the dwarf threatened to bear fruit
we thought of death, no
we thought of murder
we thought of keeping the small small love
unworthy

# plain ginger

there were days of molasses and butter
large walnuts on the cast
iron stove
sour milk and soda

days of cloves and ginger
thick batter baked slowly

the smell seems to linger in the meadow
long and dull
it sails reddish and purple
obtuse in the afternoon

the taste of cream
the claws of innocence
and i would remain in the fescue to see it again

the iron of having known you
the claws of what is always lost

the days that were here once
you swallowed
with your wide-open eyes

## chili pine

tender, the tree stands
in need of shade
burrowing in the sub-soil
lilting at the edges

portrait of a young tree
hangs in the hallway of my past
far from its native mountains

i can view it from the old orchard
where the cock's foot furrows
long and folded
fine and purple

tender, the present absence
the need to live introduced
on irrigated pastures

why is it so hard to grow wild
tell me, lacerated
wild one, let me know
how to run from the long halls of those pines

BED
OF
OPIUM

**I**

all i am is a rocky coast
nothing more

where they still make dip-candles
melted tallow and warm water

where i learned patience
how time congeals

to dip them again and again
watch them grow

where salt water still licks the stones
wears them down and where

holding the candles they still
stare out on the sea

**2**

you are from the eastern fjords
you overwinter here in
what they call the new
world

a shelter from the raw
life of cows and sheep
blue-green nights, bristly
dawn grasses, copper

lamp evenings, cod
liver oil, seal oil
horse-fat and cotton-grass
wicks on fire, images

of what they call the old
world

that refuse to blow out
even here in the yellow
inflorescence.  you will find

your fjords, the harbour below
your family farm, on
returning in the spring

bleak, bleaker
than before.  the soot
the grounds of train-oil
the black smoke, you

find too
raw, suddenly too
sharp and on that second birth

will be without a world

## 3

youngsters, we crept in the grass
dried horse dung in our hands
we rubbed into the tufts

brought the fields to life
in may and in the distance
a horse drew a muckrake

up against the crouching mountain
brooding into spring
that distinct and low-growing world

impressively large when we began
pales into purple
fragments of an image, the solid

earth will not hold
hay pastures will not green
the familiar face of our mountain

knows us no more

**4**

a month into summer, the lambs

born, sometimes died
separated at night from the ewes
there was milk

for a poor family
the week-old lamb left to find its own
early in the year

young they shot up
flowered the hillsides in twos and threes
jumped through water

tender over stony ground
they defined us well
helpless, took on

the violence of our hunger
seasons have rolled beyond the dead
it is our turn, separated

to wander alone in the barren pass

# 5

the strains of our lives
cross and recross, both of us
had our childhood feet in
field cabbages, turnips, learned
b. oleraceus by heart

the only green vegetable in the dead of the year

kales, collards, curling
leaves, folding heads.   both

had long afternoon candles, we
lit them for guests with childish
hands, the kind
chieftains burned for themselves.   both

waited while the altar candles
took flame one by one, the kind
they called the king candle
three lights in one.   both

grew to work by flame
sewing, shearing
sheep, the candle half an ell long

this is the tissue of
the green and blazing beating of
our hearts, the life
we pulled from the soil
the memory we now

kindle

## 6

we have made the days
pungent, marred winter
on the ice of clarity

we have thrown mustard
oil, made the nights
bitter.   when you reach

for me, is it because
we must always pay
for those who suffered before
that i give in?

the close rooms, charred
by the dull lamps

or do we attempt solace
at one another's hands

for that one flame
in the tallow-filled chunk of
wood that shone

in the window, you too
coming home off the mountains
dark brown wind and then

that one distant light
beyond the snow?

## 7

we only border on
the cultivated, after years of
hybrid life this is still
a wild state
we are in, it must be

memory does this
the evening wakes, winter
after autumn haying and
slaughter season, when
the wakes begin for real

to settle with the wool
catching sleep on the sly, in
the dusk between
spinning wheels, we can-
not eradicate the past
we share, the origin of

this need, to touch
here on the stream bank
pain spun into the back of our
minds, how it borders
the field of desire

## 8

how long do we keep this wake
you and i, we have no hourglass
we see no stars in the granular
texture of our time

the night may pass by us and we
still here at dawn, caught
by morning in each other's
arms.   let us

measure love the old way
how night was tallied when we
children counted stitches on
knitting needles, time struck

when the cows called for fodder
when infants yawned, when
the lýsi was burnt out and last
when the dipper showed in

the deep sky.   we can tell
from our coarse beginnings, dawns
of wholemeal and salt, when
we have seized enough

## 9

we cling to the morning, un-
willing to rise, in-
side this comfort, cattle

nudge in the hay, mixed
with field poppies
there are symptoms

our forefathers like this
within the closet of sleep
with totem-pole bedposts

the curtains that shielded
from onrush of day
hung on the spinal joints of

porbeagle sharks in the sea
the comfort in which we
were conceived

to carry over the tonic of
love, to refuse the wel-
come of daylight nar-

cosis, no.  the cattle
chew, let them wait
for the shark turns, one

more ring

**10**

you tell me think of red
poppies in summer meadows
the deep-dewed fields
think of our native soil

the extreme north
the small sleep, summer
winter, the rudeness of
work, think of

the crude bed, to lie
on mats of hay
to lie in the light-
green moss.   we both say

we will not love, the scar-
let sun, the bluish
anthers in the bloom
of desire will not show

yet our fingers touch
our arms, legs of kelp inter-
twine with a life of their
own.   is this not

love, not our
seaweed bed, are we not
home?   where sleep
escapes, where all is

extreme

## I I

kill me off, make me new
in the ashes of my life

cultivate me fresh like grapes
in a vineyard on the rolling hills
give me a world of mustard seed
a pungent life, a biting taste

make me fit for worthier things
the spice, the salt

my life has been too dark
the wakes i have kept blinded

i have spent the years in a corner
far from the flame
attempted to live by reflections
of water held to the light

my dead life has fallen about me
objects of stone, they have kept me
from moving

i want to leave them behind
walk away from the hard edges
to be matured like the mellowing
mustard in oak barrels

to age in the daylight
a life of coloured glass
of flavour, of consistency

kill this old part of me
that walks among the weeds and dust
changing as the clouds shift

bring me into the open field
the burning sky
make me new

## 1 2

let me be born in the spring
when may awakens
with charlock, yellow flowers
dark russet seeds

icebergs on the sea give way
to fogs.  when as kids
we counted worms in mud and
dandelions in grass, were

put to crumbling frost
out of horse manure, the first
work of a poor people's year
to collecting for fuel, beating

hay fields with our feet
pouring crumbs from a bucket
on the hips, stepping
slowly among the tufts

the way it was when i first
began, before the bitter mustard
oil of wealthier years arrested
the seasons.  but cattle still feed

on weeds, charlock still
cooks in milk in times of
want.  send me into the fields now
to the swans in the dark blue pond

i have kept until now
under the heart of remembrance
that time when every day was
a gift of birth

**13**

so i instruct you on
the fruit of the poppy
seeds smooth and round, how
they are released from pores and
drop

like so.  you and i
can count them one
by one, our good fortune
what we have, the

knitted bedsheets, the coarse
woolen coverlet, the ptarmigan
feather quilt.  here
we flood, come
to life

over and over throughout the night
one by one the images
we had of ourselves are
released from ob-
livion and we can

rehearse the flight of
the kittiwakes we left
behind, how they dash
one after another

into the north
atlantic foam and above
them how the red
flowers pinch the senses
in the wind

## 14

we cannot die if only
ptarmigan feathers fill our quilt
we are safe

from the sudden heart, the
seizure in bed, the
crib death of adults

we know our hunger is
the dangerous alkaloids, the
adverse effects, the

hairy leaves of our thirst
could cover us with
the linen of death.

but we are safe
the eiderdown, the sea-
birds we crawl among

nothing will touch us as
we follow this mountain trail
the ptarmigan scuttle

the fields are mild
are green, are soft and
we may eat

**15**

crush the seeds in your
hands and your fingers are
covered in oil.   this is

the substance of love.   back
home everyone slept
naked, two and three

in a bed.   space was
small then.   clothes were folded under pillows.   if

you undressed socks and shoes
together you took off
your good fortune.   i know

those poppy seeds are used
in bread in the middle
east and turkish

peasants make tonic cakes
with roasted poppy seed
olive oil and honey

we can put our fortune on
again, one foot at
a time.   your shoes

at the end of the bed
your hands that knead
the bread of life

space is wide now
large and full of unex-
plored brown stars

# NORTH
# COUNTRY
# WAKE

**I**

it must be desolation that makes us
so unfit for the world
remembrance of poverty

a courtyard in the back
i was nine, wore the same red
sweater, clogs every day.   waste

ground, black weeds fenced
the alley, low tough leaves
peppered the gravel.   my job

to take in the wash, frozen
stiff on the line.   copper
pan in a tin basin

at my feet, filled with oil and
a flame wagging under a dimming
november sky between gables

i still hold those cold sheets
against my chest, bend to lift
the bucket of light that was

to have been a lantern and
carry it inside, into the stone
cellar where we lived

**2**

for many years night would fall
closely guard the dull yellow and
grey housefronts up and down
njálsgata.   their secrets kept

some drunkard tried all the doors
stumbled into ours, down
the steps, sipped from his flask in
the washhouse, cursed under his breath

it would be black beyond
the window, we were in need of light
i was sent to fetch the fire
upstairs, open the cast iron stove

borrow a flame, bring it down
for our lamp in the wall niche
where a stick hung by a chain
to stir the wick that would fade

at the incoming air
there was one room for four of us
one lamp to study the world
atlas by, to dream

and when i did bring in the light
they would all sit up, would
greet me, the muttering drunk stagger out
and night would look up from the cobblestones

**3**

in the new grass, women
with rakes of birch scraped
the pasture into mounds

we carried winter away
where it lay in piles at the edge
of the field, in buckets

on small clogs and when summer
truly spread its fingers at the end
of the day, we received

blessings of honey cake and butter
in the kitchen where cabbage
crinkled leaves in water

we thought this a common life
the world our locale
the universe framed in our coast

shingles of rock and cliff
sands above high water mark
the margins of knowledge

with the last of the labouring
scarf-bound women
with the last broken rake

buckets abandoned to rust under
the front steps, dust settling
on the cold stove of the empty home

there is no blessing left
in the work we do, summer
arrives with no help from our hands

**4**

after shearing we washed
the wool in old urine and water
dried in sun, rinsed

in straw baskets in the stream
the washing pot at the riverside
on glowing coals, we stirred

the tangles with a stick
poured them on a raft
floating above the falls

spread out on the grass
the day's work over
there were wild vegetables

goosefoot and sea kale
in flowering bud, we had
tenderness to cultivate

bitterness to blanch
the tang of strong washes
the texture of sun-dried wool

turned into dream
the growth of a garden
we have removed from the body

bleached in the river
that falls across years
and dissipates into sea

## 5

time of taking up turf
gathering of eiderduck eggs
mending of walls

time of no ceremony

digging of ditches
flattening of fields
horses treading down the sod and

long sea voyages
barrels of pickled sea kale
coastal market towns

the prolific time, now
unfamiliar, unrecorded
away from the coasts

we import life itself
take pains to be distant
unbroken sod, untouched turf

idle horses, scrapped ships
shredded crofts.  we no
longer gather our own

sustenance

**6**

at the last, people
worked the sod, tore down
hay coverings, spread
turf on the grounds

we youngsters beat the dried clods
piled stones for cairns
carting them long ways
for wanderers in the tundra

we did not see the depletion
the precarious hold
we had on the island and
the threat of thoughtlessness

we collected thin seeds in march
on light sandy soil
we were the young shoots
earthed as we appeared

but we approach autumn
season of cutback
there is no will with us
to green-layer the ground

or gather signposts for the lost
we let it go, the wind
blows away sand, hay and
then us at last

# THE
# SILENT
# HAND

## the silent hand

we cannot be sure where
we come from.   all
that matters is

where we long to go
the silent hand that draws us
in

# I

back at the childhood piers and docks
i was looking at the whalers, a fleet of five
boats, men making them ready for a new
season.  went into the mess, out
onto the steering platform.  on the prow
in front the harpoon gun, on the mast
above the crow's nest, all
to chase down whales

when one of the crew came up, said
are you greenpeace?  i guess i didn't look
like a child of this outfit.  and i was
admittedly greenpeace yes but told him
no, i'm a poet.  which was true as far
as it went.  what are you writing?
he asked, about whales or whaling or
what?  yes, about that

he couldn't put it together, it wasn't
right for poetry, this business of
death and streams of blood, masses of
flesh.  shook his head at me, who
he said, who is going to read that?

**2**

in the half dusk that never went
dark across the whole of
the town reykjavik, the mountain esja
the depths of the fjord they called
whale fjord, hvalfjördur, my grand-
uncle rose daily imitating the weak
attempt at sunrise

all the men and women rose to one
purpose.  to open season, to go
*whaling* they said the way the ancients
went to *viking*, to sub-
sist.  in a raw morning we looked
after the ships together, the masts
going *out*

at school later in the morning
still dark, one by one the kids stood
to recite *eldgamla ísafold*.  bored
flipping pages i landed
on the faeroe islands, faereyjar
*grindadráp í faereyjum*.  all of them

men, women and children in the water
beating in the small whales with bare
hands, herding them in
the ocean red with blood as far
as you looked.  the returning
question, what is cruelty, when
do you choose not to
subsist

**3**

5 a.m., ready to go
on the ship the lights
were on, the men tightening
leather straps around sweaters and socks
books and oilskins, against the lamps
on board the snow flurried
confused and angry

i looked at the sea, that open
black mouth of storm and
waves, then down
at the open boat rocking vio-
lently, knocking against the pier
palm of what hand is this?
slowly we saw

the boat glide, the hand
harpoons and arrows trace out the night
search for dawn and whale.  the rest
had to be imagined, how
they didn't see him but sensed
the huge presence.  words

voices i still hear
telling us the story of how we were
saved.  we could have starved
to death.  it was whale
that saw us through.  i still think

this is the way mythologies are made

**4**

it was those long black mornings
at school i remember most
vividly, the absence of trawlers on
the banks and whalers out. my friends
whose fathers and brothers and uncles were
*out*, on the hunt they said

those kids lived the life of icebergs, you saw only little of the real
pain.  the ship may not return
there were nightmares, the lonely kitchen
where mom gazed the evening out
through the window.  Absence

absence is what i remember best
you felt it in the air you breathed, in
the eyes that looked at you, in the songs
they made us sing
the music teacher trying to cheer us
Lift your spirit Lift.  but it always
sounded dead.

Death.  seemed so near at hand

## 5

in the mornings early they dropped
the papers at the bus stop
on the other side of the beach rocks
the snow always wet, the wind wet
the papers wet, the world soaking.
a time when you beat against the half-
rain, half-snow in rubber boots

the pack of papers heavy
with slush, the effort beyond en-
durance carrying them on your back.
the mind forgets pain, with the years
it melts.   there are moments the body
disowns, slogging along the length of
kársnesbraut and kópavogsbraut in the dark

those were years when never enough
clothes and shoes existed, my face
whipped red by the ocean storm
head cold into the brain and toes
gone.  i no longer recall
the feeling.   what i do

remember is the sorrow, the whining
wind between walls, moaning in
off the sea following me.  wading up
to the door of every house, stuffing
a paper through the slot with numb
hands, wet mittens.  bringing the news
from the fishing banks.  in those days
even to be a carrier of

newspapers was to be
a messenger of death

**6**

zoology, dýrafraedi, was all
whales, drawn in hand, how
to know each one, what trade-
marks, where the lines.   we sat on boxes
in fanney's living room, memorized
each one.   the house

unfinished, raw concrete, mud and
planks up to the door. seven kids
shared the three bedrooms, fanney
slept in the bathtub.   the house was
never finished. the father was
gone, they said he

went out on the fleet and he
*became out.*
which is to *remain out.*   sometimes
i dared to imagine what actually
happens to you.   the cold water, cramps
probably instant freeze and yet
somehow consciousness remains, never

quits haunting
the book in my lap, the fine-drawn
pencil lines, a whale looking at you
oddly intelligent.   and what if
he was lost not to the sea but
to whale, what
happens to you then.   this i didn't
pursue

## 7

met him in the bookstore, he hardly
dared look up, cowered over the spines
of books facing up on the table
looking for material for the next
*tour* they called the
hunt.  i shook his elbow, uncle

unnsteinn, surprised to see you
didn't know the boat was in, he was
glad to see me, very glad yes
and i remember thinking how much like
a fugitive, unnsteinn

was the one who never left
the boat.  when they were in harbour
he stayed on board, refused
to land.  he had the radio
in his cabin and books, what more
is there.  until he needed more material

he was the one missing at
christmas and easter, all the others met
up.  it was a seasonal pull, two
or three making one more trip
to the dock, one more attempt to
persuade unnsteinn out.  but i knew
he was afraid of land

## 8

there were the long weeks when vigdís
never came to school.  the streets
were empty, the village abandoned.  i
saw no sense to the rocks and grime
she locked herself in her room, the
small attic where she dreamed
apparitions of a newly dead father

tried to piece the story together, another tour, a hunt gone
wrong.  men caught in the ropes
that pulled in whale, slid
as the aft opened to let the monster
in

but none of the dramatics came home
just a slow boat, a missing presence
vigdís taking wrong turns from then on
if eyes could scream i thought i'd hear hers
loudly.  there was the silent house
when she asked me home, the heavy
clock, the weight of the air, the message
not to speak

**9**

the truth is, sjana mín, that whales
are capable of love, uncle stefán
said who used to pilot the boats before his wife asked him to stay
home, she couldn't take the pain of
not knowing and his answer then, you do
everything for your wife

i've been out there, i've seen
what happens he said.  we were in
the loft, the ship models he'd built
since he went on land were on the shelves
the window looking out on the fjord
always that rusty trawler lay below
in the sand, barnacles and seaweed on
the hulk at low tide

the whale knows how it is with us, how
crops won't grow, clouds won't break
the herring won't come.  he knows when
the nets are empty and appears instead
i've seen that huge mass swim towards us
lift his head before the harpoon
gun and wait.  there was a time it struck me

the men shot.  i couldn't have
done it.  absolutely sure he had volunteered
himself, that's the truth

THE
NIGHT WORKERS
OF
RAGNARÖK

# the rest of mankind

i have tried to account for the future
untie it
maybe the disturbing factor is simple
atomic energy
i cannot say

i should only be concerned
in black and white
about power used to eradicate
even the lumpsucker boy
from raufarhöfn who peers out

through ropes and chains
of the rigging on his "sigurvon"
in a black and white wool sweater
as he ties down the sail
i know

the season is good, 1800
kilos in a day
and the white chest of a small
duck crosses the black water
and glides behind the wheelhouse

but this is a topic that has to be
introduced
a little better
and there is time, of course
since i often cut across the docks

## an involvement of lattices

on wednesday it occurs to me
when workers in hafnarfjördur
hang up fish
for drying on racks in kapelluhraun

i could formulate something
in the way of an either-or
such as will all that power—
enough to eliminate a couple
of cities to start with—

be used to clear up
the problems of existence
or not?  in the meantime
the ground under the fish racks
looks exceedingly black

and the workers' oilskins very yellow
so late in the day
i have been staring too long
at the city of the dead in kapelluhraun
where stockfish is made

how the people shuffle up and down
among the lattices, small
explosive suns, seen
with black patches on the eyes

at least on wednesday
it occurs to me to find
the matter of drying out in early spring
simple

## in the meantime

i often think there is no ground
even for poetry
it could happen
things do go wrong

they say it is uncertain
even if the future contains survivors
that anyone will care
for culture then

i see they are moving telephone
poles in hornafjördur
a distant country of escape
where birds with naked breasts
beat grey wings fast
and then sail
away

125 kilometers covered
on 1400 poles, 3 tons each
375 kilometers of wire
132 thousand volts

i often think how heavy
it is
to say a few words
or even listen
to the hawk of the soul

# when one thinks

we thrive and develop, at least
so far, by burning
oil and coal, reservoirs stubby and short
that will not last
nothing lasts
we too are exhaustible

in another generation or so
nothing is left of the accessible
and they say we will use what we get
in getting it

even the fish are reserved
already in march they refuse
to come to the hornafjördur boats
and gudmundur skipper complains
about easter
he prefers fish

says the haddock cannot be tempted by a line after christmas
and by march the rest
swallow capelin
and go to sleep on the ocean floor

all the boats between hvalnes
and west to ingólfshöfdi
look forward to april
when the fish wake up
and long to look at the sun

from afar in the water
a burning sun of the sea parrot—
for some this is
a horrifying perspective
at least, so far

# directions over the phone

the woman in strönd called

six months pregnant, way out

in munadarnes by ingólfsfjördur
in snow
in poor visibility
and the coastguard sends a helicopter
into uncertainty

we all follow

the progress, waiting by the radio
and outside the window a chicken-like
creature wobbles heavily, the bad
wind booms and blows
across the opening of a coke bottle

stub after stub fills the ashtrays
as if it were us
waiting for rescue, we spend the time
wondering about year 2000
we all know by then the earth's
population will be twice
what it is now

and the hollow voice in the machine

says the doctor consulted
over the telephone
and the helicopter is forced to turn back

there is no way
you can make it through that weather

## this is for our own use

god swallows a lot of snow
in fljótsdalshérad
the weather tumbles into the garden
unasked, in sharp shoes
with squall and snowheaps

on such days i wonder if it is time

to find new sources of energy
perhaps our own
the energy of beasts
wind and water should cover the bare
necessities they say
in part

this is not an exhausted issue
the day i turn 33 all
the roads from hérad to the sea
close
the school kids have to turn around
and workers fight their way to work

i hear in 1950
the combined power of man and beast
all over the world
amounted to 150 million hp.
we agree that is nothing
next to the 3 billion of machines

be that as it may
on my birthday I notice the field
marks around egilsstadir
are snowmobiles and plows

unclogging the passage from door to door

## it has been hectic

the worker describes something
with those big hands
in the processing plant
yellow and blue grime sticks to the table
and the iron crates are full of heads

describes perhaps how to use the sun
directly and another
lifts a strip of fish
and looks the other way
because there are no signs of solar energy yet
and you scale what you have

this room is no ordinary work
of art, piles of fish
fill the floor like water
halfway up the stairs
and just as in splitting atoms
there is nowhere to put your foot
when the catch is good

twelve times in the last week
i have passed those buckets of heads
pink and purple in the march gust
where the three-toed smell of fish
is a peaceful objective

and every time i am reminded
that which threatens, protects

# fell down the stairs and died

until further notice
one is free to go over the facts:

1951—an atomic reactor makes electricity
1954—in russia an atomic plant
1955—nautilus
1956—calder hall, england
but this is enough

otherwise
when spring is young the birds
fly weakly over the marsh
without pattern
and drop fast
their wings almost black
and collapsible

there are low rapid calls in the marsh
that cannot be heard
for the moment
one experiment follows another
and the technical difficulties sponge
into the air like summer
warmer every day

soon we can take off our sweaters

# the practical uses of atomic energy

now and then the weather lets up
the shrimp fishers swear
rowing out on arnarfjördur is a dream
on such days

deckhands in bíldudalur can be heard
familiar as the long strings of geese
migrating overhead

but even those birds do not escape
large new problems
and we are always deceived

## it will also be necessary

one day this winter
a boy drove a car
up from downtown
and got as far as skúlagata at the harbour

at this point in the story
i wonder what happens next
when all the uranium is gone
(in 1960 they claimed what we had
would only do another generation)

or whether there is in other words
more material
perhaps of another kind
as to the boy

he lost control of the wheel
rammed into a parked car
(across from the radio station in fact)
skidded across the street
onto the sidewalk
and into the sea

theoretically one may end this
in various ways
but they all require solving
innumerable mathematical deficiencies
not that one should not try on one's own

he was alone in the car
he crawled out of the open window
swam up
and stood dripping on the street in the night

## nothing realistic

in april, time of dusky wings
and black tails on the buoys
siglufjördur lies suffocating
under snow

truckers give a fifty percent cut
to shift winter about
people take to their horses
and something else arises
nuclear waste

but the future is too wide
to consider these things
and in siglufjördur the expenses of processing uranium
are of no account
there is no nuclear energy
no waste
nothing

but a cluster of black horsemen
waiting on hvanneyrarbraut
for a snow-filled truck
to pass them by

later, mind you
the summer flocks are sure to arrive

## those subjected to radioactivity who did not die were marked for life

the idea of storing
nuclear waste in the sea once had
a strong following
but i understand
there is not enough water in all the oceans
to cover even ten percent of our sins

today a black-capped bird
eats flies at the landing place
a young gull circles
with a rasping call

the lumpsucker season started
the day before yesterday
freshly caught fish lie
in a wagon outside the shed
and a little girl sells them, her hands folded

i hear
the banks from skagatá to langanes are open
and northern boats are out on the cold sea
too cold, they say
and the lumpsucker is late this year

again sounds the za-za of the gull
down by the broken boards
and rusty nails
today i feel particularly aware
of the possibility

that radioactivity resembles sin
it spreads unseen
through plankton, algae, fish
and i have come to buy it from a little girl
with folded hands

## and useless you will become

the chunky ducks
flap into tjörnin, the town pond
on the water the tails spread
pleased with the fresh water

they try to drown themselves
stick their heads as deep as they can
but float
like persistent balloons

i wish we had some of that buoyancy
after all the disasters at sea this year
one eats fish with reverence

or i wish markús had been born earlier
the net-braider in hafnarfjördur
who invented a way of saving the sorrowful
sailors from drowning
when they fall overboard
the markús net is thrown into the sea
and see
they have become fishers of men

things are not always obvious
even a slight exposure to low levels
of radioactive rays, they say
involves genetic mutations
in the future
and see
the sins of the parent are visited on the child

how i wish markús really had a net
like the one simon peter threw out
and the boat became heavily loaded
with the good

## with the help of science

if you do not remember the little birds

flaps of narrow stiff wings
in the snow-troughs
of deep winter
they will surely die

when the dark flocks bounce
like frozen ping-pong balls
in the cluster of birdseed
you threw into the parking lot

stories of the survival of the fittest
need not concern you
one would suppose natural selection
put the birdseed into your hand
so they would not die

one even supposes the old theory is unnatural
we know we can extend life
otherwise doomed to failure
at the brush of a hand

# icebound on february 25

today is the dead of winter
when the mind is arrested
by the harbour at ísafjördur

to find it chained in ice
once more

no political understanding
no euratom, cern, nordic institute
no mutual moderation, as they say

can open those unkind hands
that scrape the white paint
off the patient hulls

or dampen that rich
dark voice, the north-eastern wind
that litters the decks

with tiny mites of impossibility

## the night the moon fell

winter shearing is almost over
in february and march
if the sheep cot is warm
and the feeding trough is full
the sheep are plucked clean

in south langholt there is no problem
the farmers learn from each other
to shear at least eighty in a day
with electric shears

this is a new tradition
it came with the birds of autumn
and i have never seen a naked sheep
in winter before

i do not envy those who go naked

never before have i seen the seabirds
wheel so over the waves
in wide circles
like half-moons on their side
that drop into the water

and i believe the world sleeps
facing the window

## cakes and ale for the deceased

this evening a slim grey bird
flies erratically high
over the roofs of the city
"bird of dusk
blow up my superstition"
it is a deep tradition
to address birds as they bomb down
before the ingrown window in one's wall

"lies, falsehoods, blast them
in the poor-wills of the night
when the tomcats look up from the alley
round-eyed and jerky"

i do not stand by the window and wish
mistrust into the grave
i know the birds do not perch
on trees when there are none
"jumpy flyer over the fishermen's school

today glaumur searches for hot
water, 31° C
he drills into grundarfjördur
180 meters down and truly
glaumur will go further
he will hew and burrow down a thousand meters to avoid the
                                            thought of war"

the bird of dusk is blotted out by distance

that is usually when i wonder when
the age of victory
passed away

## may 1 in grandagardur

the day they forbade the children
to clean the beaches with their hands
because they would be harmed
by pollution

i went down to the wooden shacks
where the small-time fishers
polish up the open boats
for spring fishing

may was in the old men's lungs
and down by the water
where rusty tin cans lay among the rocks
i heard a reedy song

by chance
a little gurgling voice
that grew into a guttural rattle
and when the brothers ran their plastic boat into the sea

i knew they will be using old words
long after they have lost their meaning

# this

in vestmannaeyjar they count their wealth
in codheads with a knife
as the nights become edged with white
the rich rip apart their silver
cod, haddock, black pollack

they stand in the night in their aprons
and lattices are built on the ledges beyond
in april they say
it rains fish on the islands

i have seen the yellow neck of the sky
i have seen evening and morning undulate into one

no other world shows so much white
and as the painter's hand brushes
red streaks onto the south-eastern sky
after eight

i should like to go to vestmannaeyjar again
and count my gold
in the sun that refuses to leave

because I know the earth is a place
where you cannot hurt a fish-working girl
without the consequences bleeding out
like a gash in the throat
of a world that sings

## night workers

night after night in ísafjördur
they don't take off their working clothes
and they don't say anything for long
after the fire

if they prefer flowers
in the garden when the sun glows
they waste no words on what might have been
after the fire

stopping only for black
coffee by the gudný's charred hull
they think no more of soccer on the grass
after the fire

the electricians and machinists
hand to hand, before and after
the flame of midnight they keep on
After the fire, they say

she'll be rowing again in three mornings
because they stay
gutting away the burnt insides
and replacing day with day